WYOM

A BOOK OF 21 POS

MW00436902

BROWNTROUT PUBLISHERS
SAN FRANCISCO • CALIFORNIA

BROWNTROUT PUBLISHERS

P.O. BOX 280070
SAN FRANCISCO • CALIFORNIA 94128-0070

ISBN: 1-56313-859-X
TITLE #: P6859

BROWNTROUT publishes a large line of calendars, photographic books, and postcard books.
Please write for more information.

Printed in Hong Kong

WYOMING
Barn and Grand Tetons

BROWNTROUT PUBLISHERS • SAN FRANCISCO, CALIFORNIA

WYOMING
Hay bales in Star Valley below Salt River Range in autumn

PUBLISHED BY BROWNTROUT • SAN FRANCISCO, CALIFORNIA

WYOMING

Upper Geyser Basin with steam venting from Castle Geyser,
Yellowstone National Park

PUBLISHED BY BROWNTROUT • SAN FRANCISCO, CALIFORNIA

WYOMING
Aspen in autumn along Darwin Creek, Targhee National Forest

PUBLISHED BY BROWNTROUT • SAN FRANCISCO, CALIFORNIA

WYOMING
Temple Peaks, Bridger Wilderness, Wind River Range

PUBLISHED BY BROWNTROUT • SAN FRANCISCO, CALIFORNIA

WYOMING
Mixed grass prairie, Thunder Basin National Grassland,
Campbell County

PUBLISHED BY BROWNTROUT • SAN FRANCISCO, CALIFORNIA

WYOMING
Sunflowers and peaks, Grand Teton National Park

PUBLISHED BY BROWNTROUT • SAN FRANCISCO, CALIFORNIA

WYOMING
Salt River Range seen from Prater Mountain,
Bridger-Teton National Forest

PUBLISHED BY BROWNTROUT · SAN FRANCISCO, CALIFORNIA

WYOMING
Midway Geyser Basin, Yellowstone National Park

PUBLISHED BY BROWNTROUT • SAN FRANCISCO, CALIFORNIA

WYOMING
Rock figures, Wind River Range

PUBLISHED BY BROWNTROUT • SAN FRANCISCO, CALIFORNIA

WYOMING
Snow on sagebrush, Bighorn Basin, south of Cody

PUBLISHED BY BROWNTROUT • SAN FRANCISCO, CALIFORNIA

WYOMING
Bighorn Mountains

PUBLISHED BY BROWNTROUT • SAN FRANCISCO, CALIFORNIA

WYOMING
Young Ponderosa Pine frames Devil's Tower National Monument

PUBLISHED BY BROWNTROUT • SAN FRANCISCO, CALIFORNIA

WYOMING

Horses graze in summer evening light along Popo Agie River
below Wind River Range, by Lander

PUBLISHED BY BROWNTROUT • SAN FRANCISCO, CALIFORNIA

WYOMING
Bison along Soda Butte Creek, Yellowstone National Park

PUBLISHED BY BROWNTROUT • SAN FRANCISCO, CALIFORNIA

WYOMING
View at Island Lake

PUBLISHED BY BROWNTROUT • SAN FRANCISCO, CALIFORNIA

WYOMING
Rabbit brush, Big Horn Mountains

PUBLISHED BY BROWNTROUT • SAN FRANCISCO, CALIFORNIA

WYOMING
Old cabin near Encampment in the Sierra Madre Range looking to
Medicine Bow Mountains

PUBLISHED BY BROWNTROUT • SAN FRANCISCO, CALIFORNIA

WYOMING
Sandstone formations with the Laramie Range beyond,
near Casper

PUBLISHED BY BROWNTROUT • SAN FRANCISCO, CALIFORNIA

WYOMING
Yellowstone National Park

PUBLISHED BY BROWNTROUT • SAN FRANCISCO, CALIFORNIA

WYOMING
Snake River, Grand Teton National Park

PUBLISHED BY BROWNTROUT • SAN FRANCISCO, CALIFORNIA